Bangkok Noir in New York

by
Chris Coles

Bangkok Noir in New York
Copyright @ 2019 by Chris Coles

Singapore Art Books
Suite 420, Young Place
Sukhumvit Soi 23
Klongtoey Nua, Wattana
Bangkok, Thailand 10110

www.bangkoknoir.com

No part of this publication may be reproduced, stored in a retrieval system or transmitted, in any form or by any means, electornic, mechanical, photocopying, recording or otherwise, without the prior permission of the copyright owner.

Chris Coles
Bangkok Noir in New York / Chris Coles
ISBN: 9781795051590
1. Bangkok. 2. Noir. 3. Nightlife. 4. New York. 5. Chris Coles. 6. Southeast Asia.

My 1st Exhibition in New York back in February, 2006, was modest, 20 small paintings from my Bangkok Night series. Part of a group show at an art gallery in New York's Chelsea Art District.

A major show in New York is a mountain still to climb. While some of the gallery owners liked my paintings, until the prices of the paintings gets up into the thousands, showing them and selling them in New York doesn't even cover their sky high rent and expenses.

A very successful gallery owner told me not to worry about getting a prestige New York gallery, just focus on becoming a well-known "name". Once I'm a "name", the prestige galleries will come to me.

"You clearly have a very defined, interesting style, the visual talent. And a strong vision. Just keep painting!"

Since then I've had a number of shows. In Singapore, Bangkok (where I'm based), and Phnom Penh, received quite a lot of press/media attention, even had few tv shows/documentaries feature my work, as well as several books of my paintings from the Bangkok Night.

Some day, I'll even get back to New York!

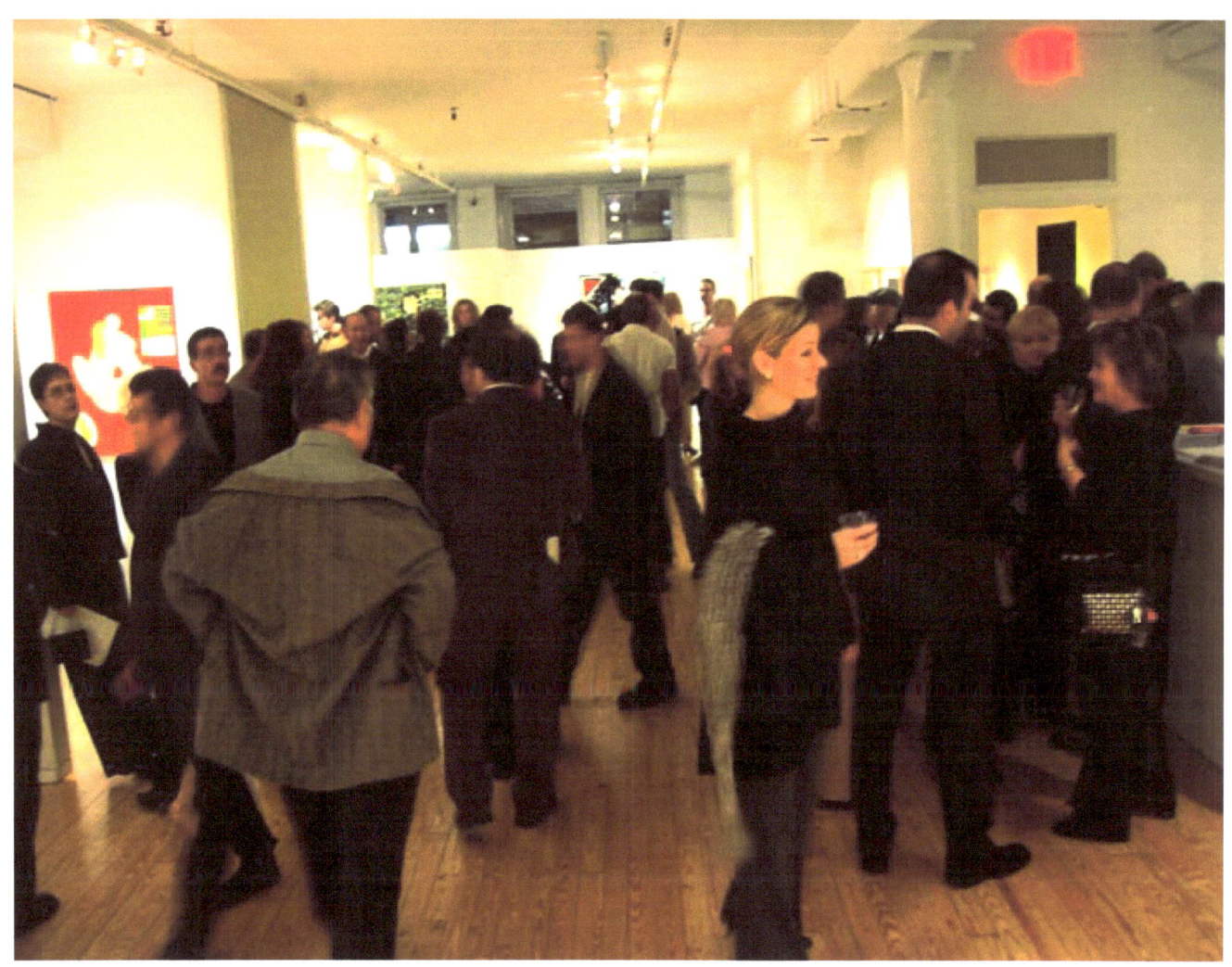

The Opening Night in New York drew a nice crowd. New Yorkers treat Art Openings kind of the same as going to a movie or a play, a civilized night out...

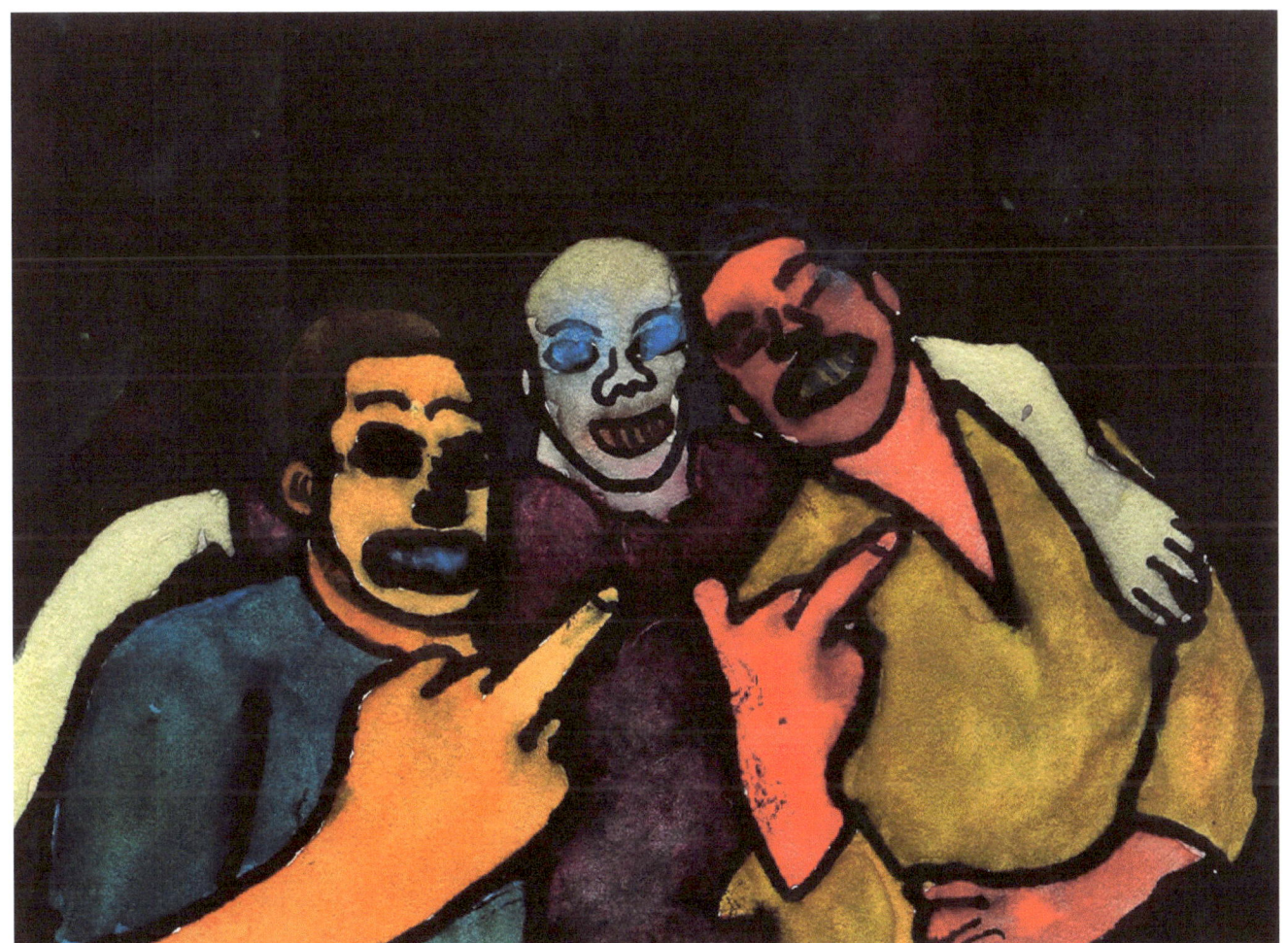

German Sex Tourists, (water color on paper, 7x5 inch)

Three German sex tourists, in Thailand on a two week package that will take them to Nana, Pattaya, Chiang Mai and Phuket. One or two girls a night for fourteen nights, plenty of beer and Fuck You to anyone who cares. It's a long cold winter in Berlin and party time in the hot Bangkok night.

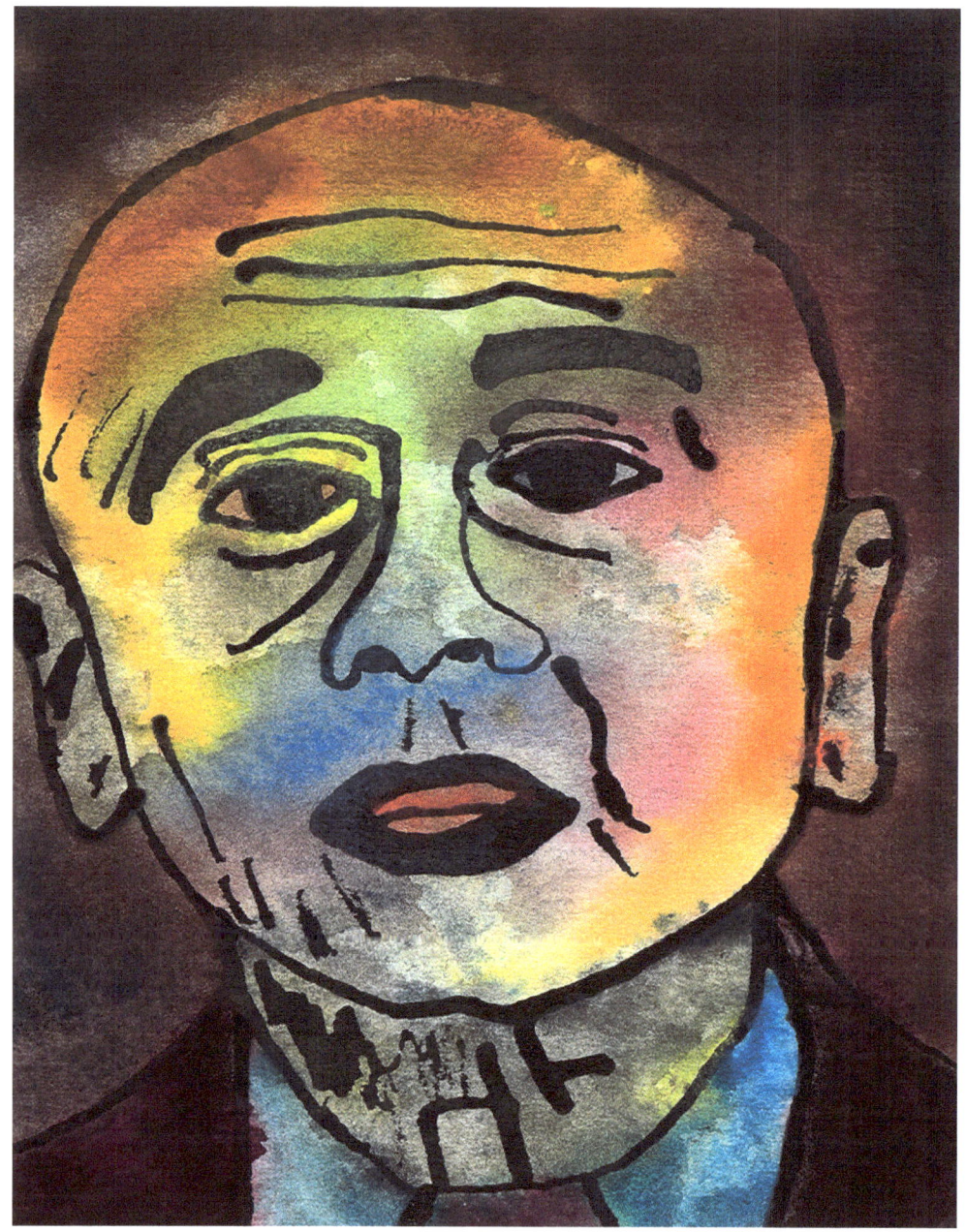

Battle-scarred Expat (water color on paper, 5x7 inch)

In Asia for thirty years, Hong Kong, Jakarta, Singapore, Shanghai, Saigon and Bangkok. The grown-up children from his first marriage back in Sydney, his first wife, their mother, a distant memory. No matter how much beer or how bald, he's still a player and will be until the day he dies. Worldly and cosmopolitan, he has already led so many lives, he's lost count.

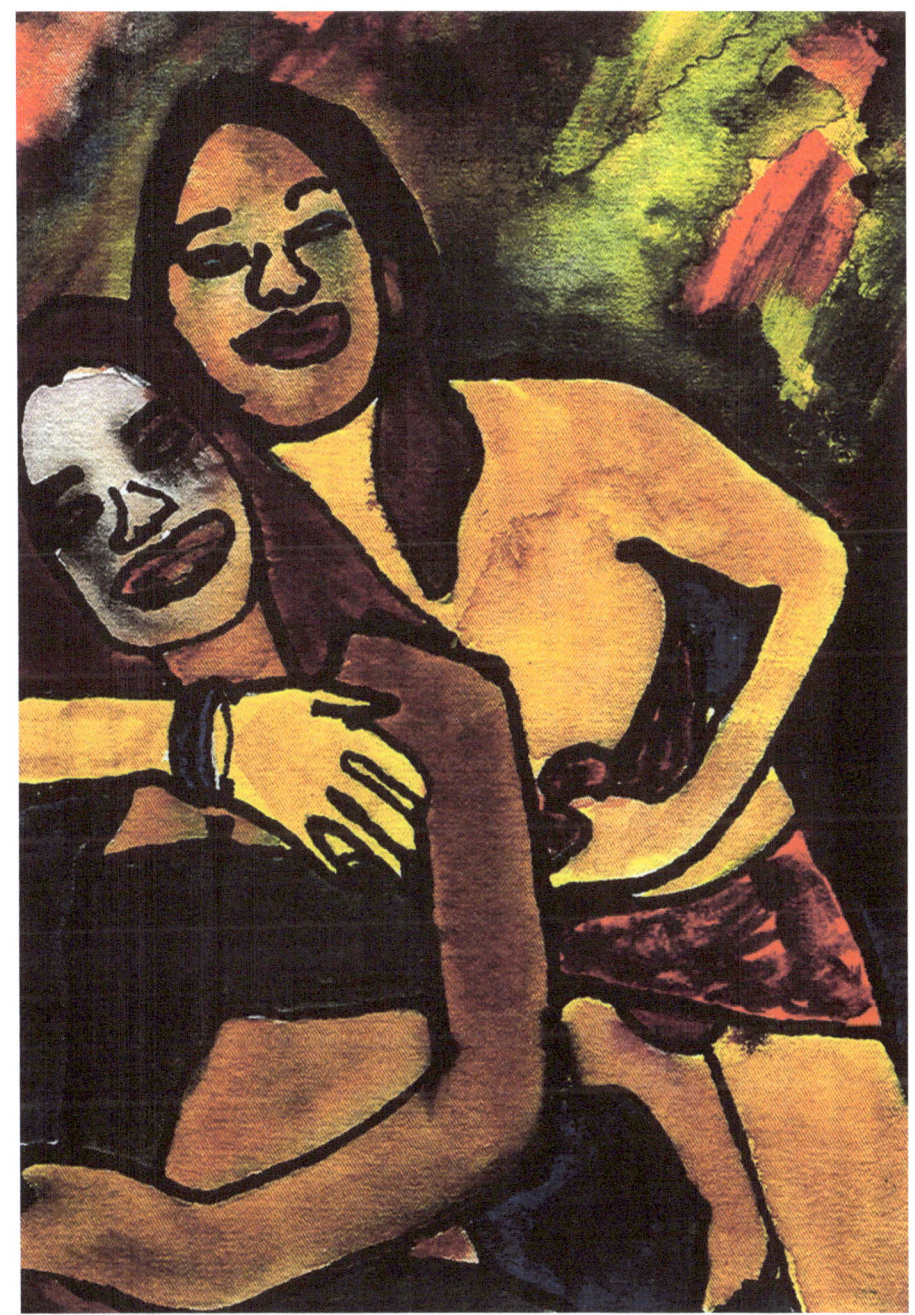

Showing Off (water color on paper, 5x7 inch)

A couple of Isan bargirls looking for attention, trying to provoke, bored and predatory.

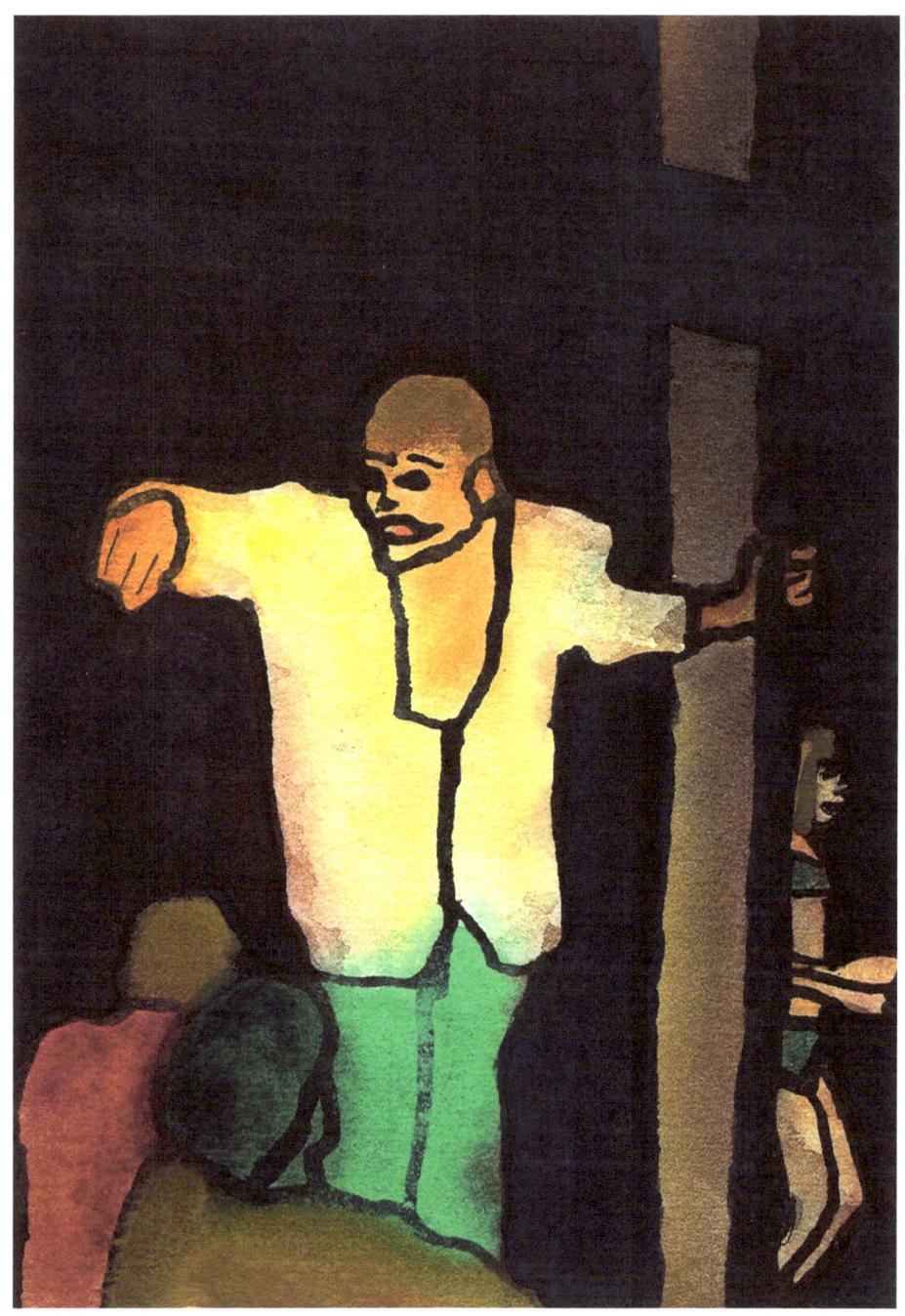

Ronnie at Nana Plaza (water color on paper, 5x7 inch)

His first year in Bangkok, a great job, big salary, living allowance, penthouse condo, even a driver……and the excitement of Nana Plaza and the Bangkok Night still alive and fresh.

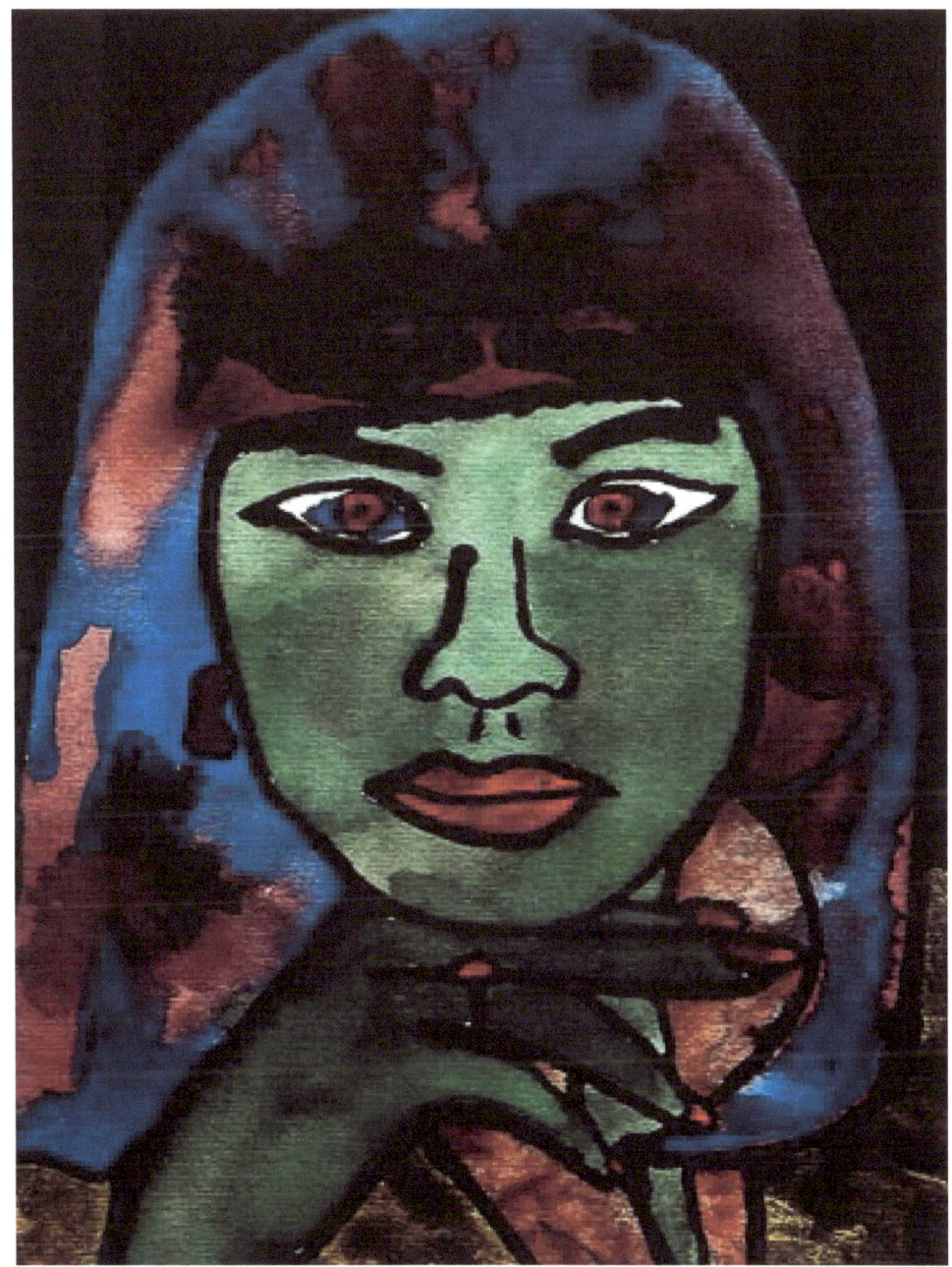

Jundee (waterrcolor 5x7 inch)

An Isan nightclub singer with a lovely voice who performs in the Morlam/Lao style from Northeast Thailand. Tall, slender, long curving hands and fingers so beautiful for the Morlam-style of dancing. A little bit Hindu, a hint of maleness and ambiguity. In Thailand, you are often not sure.

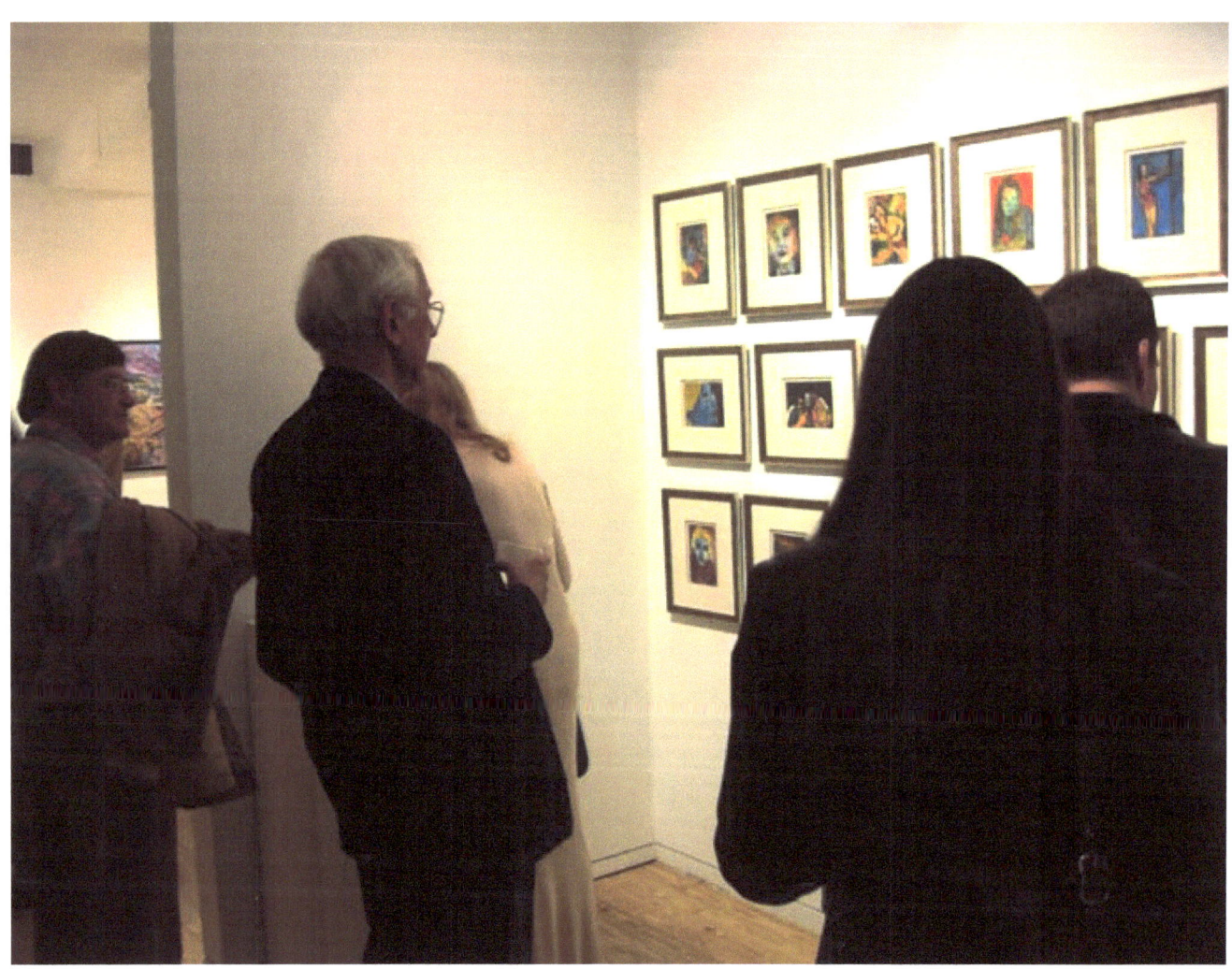
Most New Yorkers, especially New Yorkers who go to Art Shows, have never been out in the Bangkok Night or been touched by the Bangkok Night's infinity of Noir. Some of them seemed to contemplate the paintings quite carefully, studying them one by one.

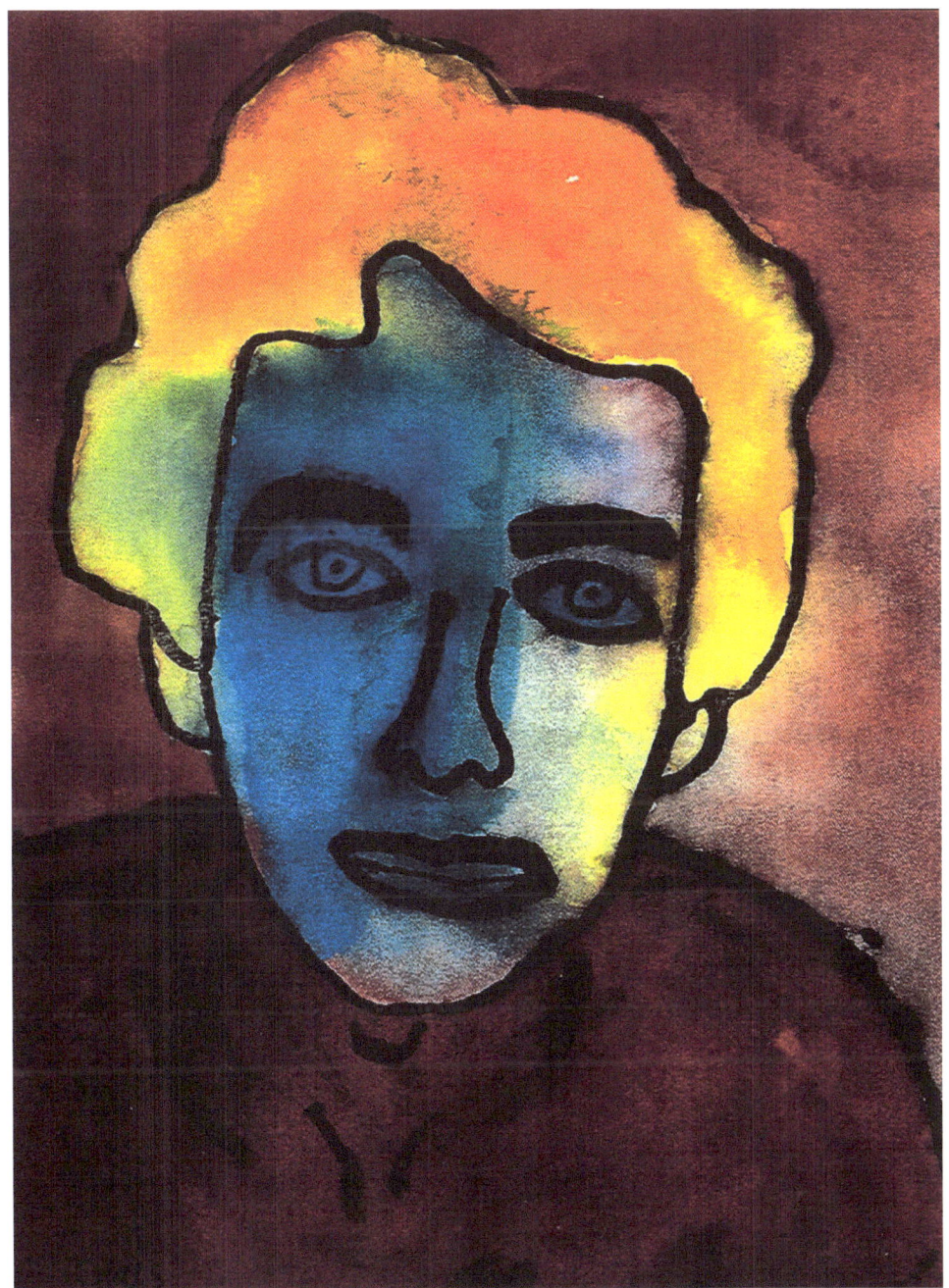

Young Blond Expat (water color on paper, 5x7 inch)

Young and handsome, the Young Blond Expat is a prize Bangkok possession. He has so many female options, he ends up confused and lost, a combination sex object and ATM, where do the girlfriends start and end, struggling to find his focus.

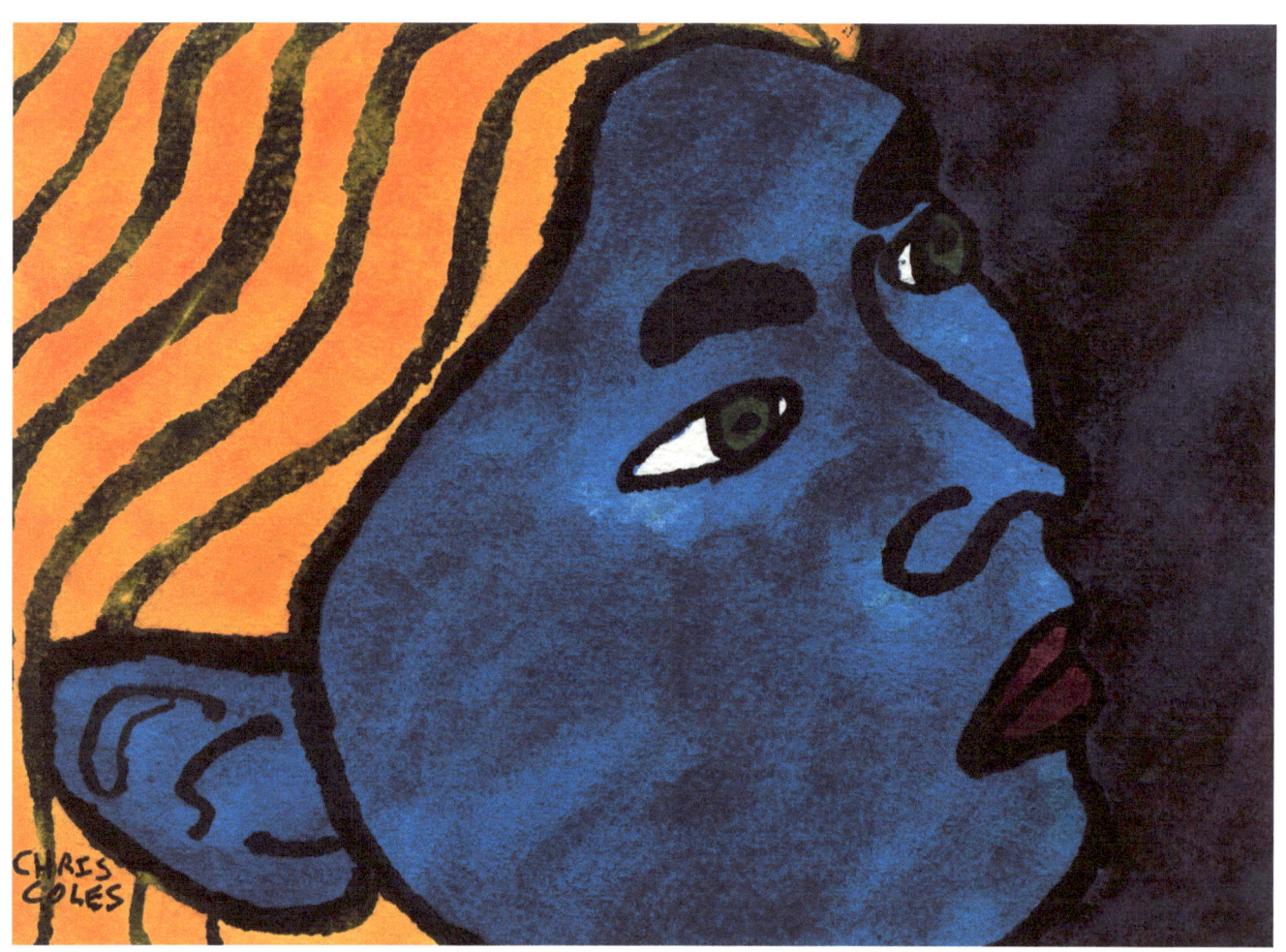

Lai (water color on watercolor paper, 7x5 inch)

Lai came to Bangkok from Ubon near the border with Cambodia when she was eighteen. She was recruited to work at a Soi Cowboy bar after she won a local beauty contest. Her monthly salary is eight thousand Baht but so many men want her, she sometimes makes as much as forty thousand Baht a month. In two years, she's had hundreds of men, a few of them more than once. So many men, she's lost track of who they are and how they look. Already, she has built a new house for her family back in Ubon and bought a pickup truck for her father and brother.

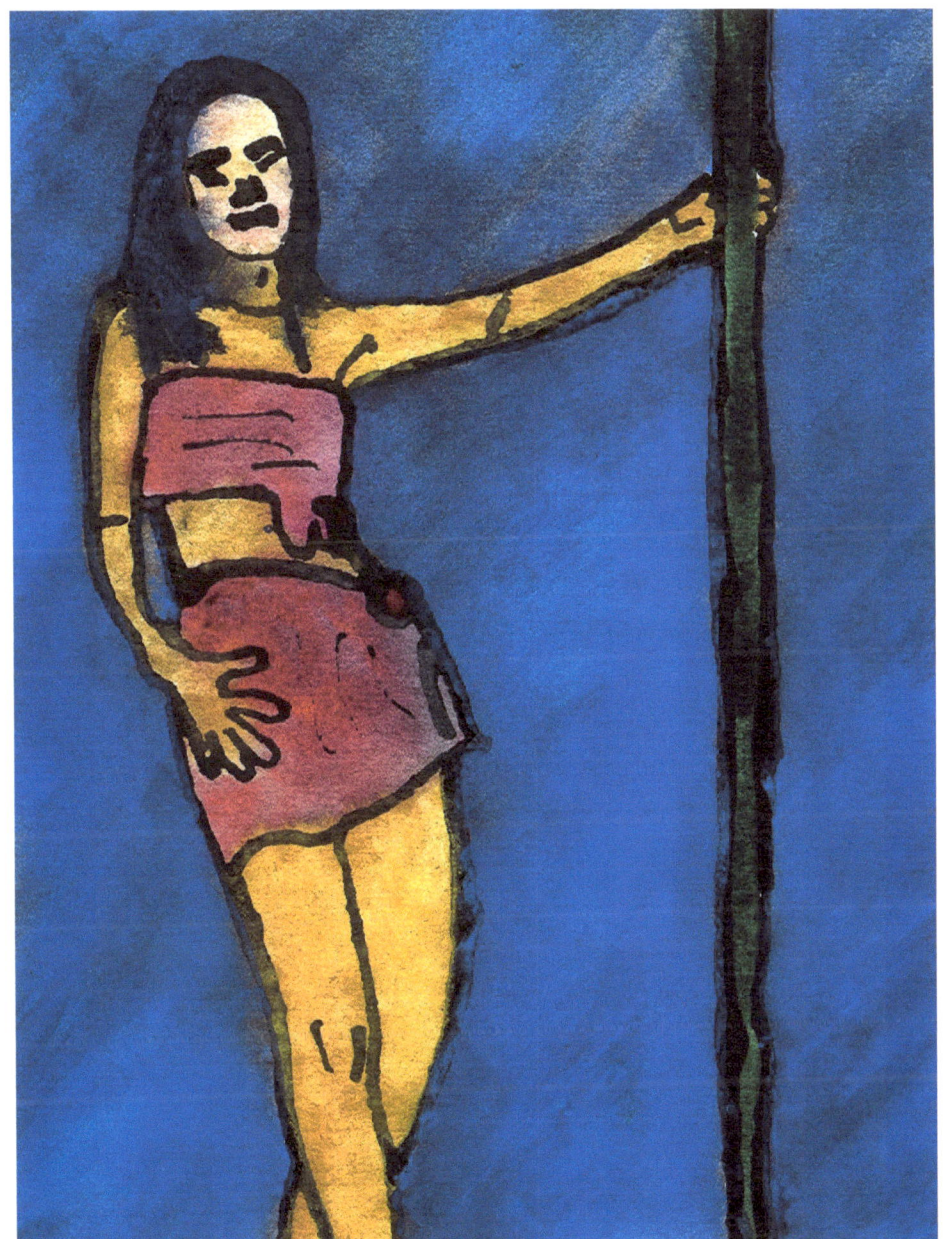

Lek at Pretty Lady (watercolor on paper, 5x7 inch)

Almost thirty, Lek's body is still slender and supple. But she has seen too much, known too many men, danced too many nights. Her only desire is to go back to her hometown, take care of her ten year old son and live out the rest of this life in quiet, hoping the next cycle will be better.

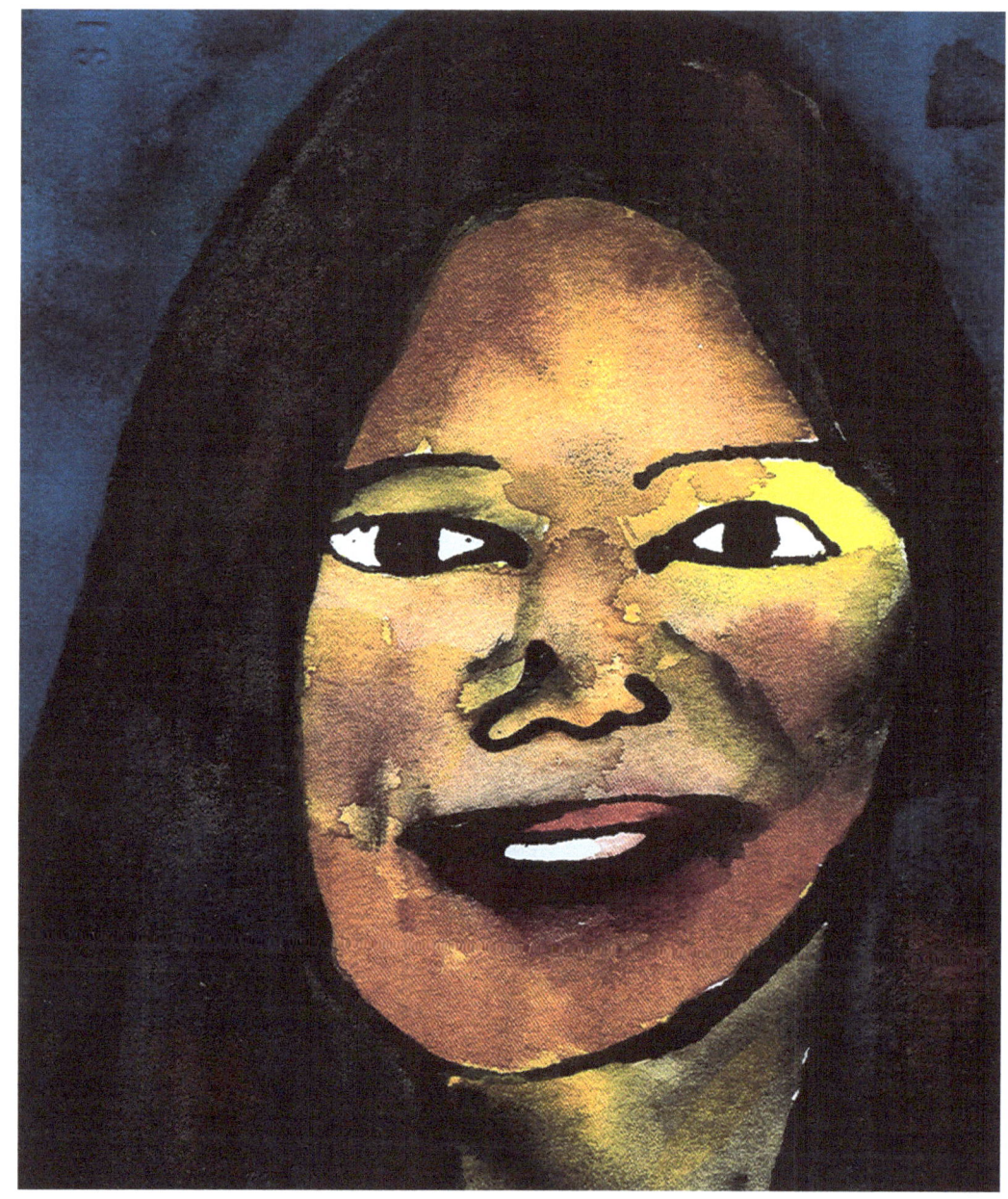

Neng (water color on paper, 5x7 inch)

For two years, Neng assembled DVD players at an electronics factory in the Rayong Industrial zone, making 7000 Baht each month, her son with her mother upcountry. Then her father became ill and stopped work. In Thailand, there's no pension plan, unemployment insurance or disability, only the family, especially the eldest daughter. She went to work in Doll House on Soi Cowboy, where her monthly take home is 30,000 Baht. Her life in shreds, she, her son and family will survive. At least for now.

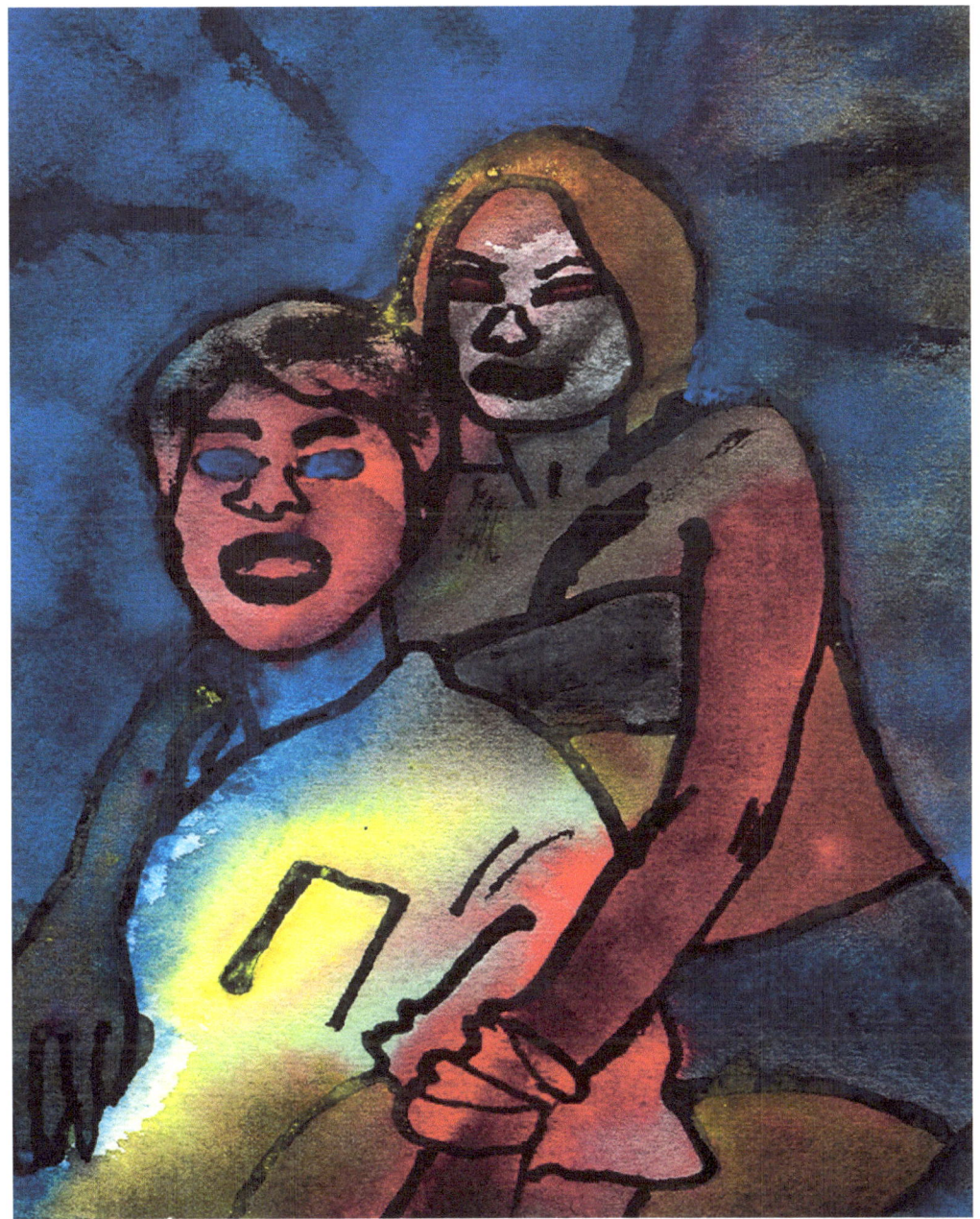

Jackpot (water color on paper, 5x7 inch)

Tonight she's hit the jackpot. Next month's rent, school fees for her son and daughter, money to send to her mother, a chance to pay off the Indian loan shark. Her guy's from Australia, in Bangkok for the first time, fresh, excited by what he sees. He's come to the bar every night for four nights, paid the bar fine and taken her to his room. He may be an awkward lover but she loves him just the same.

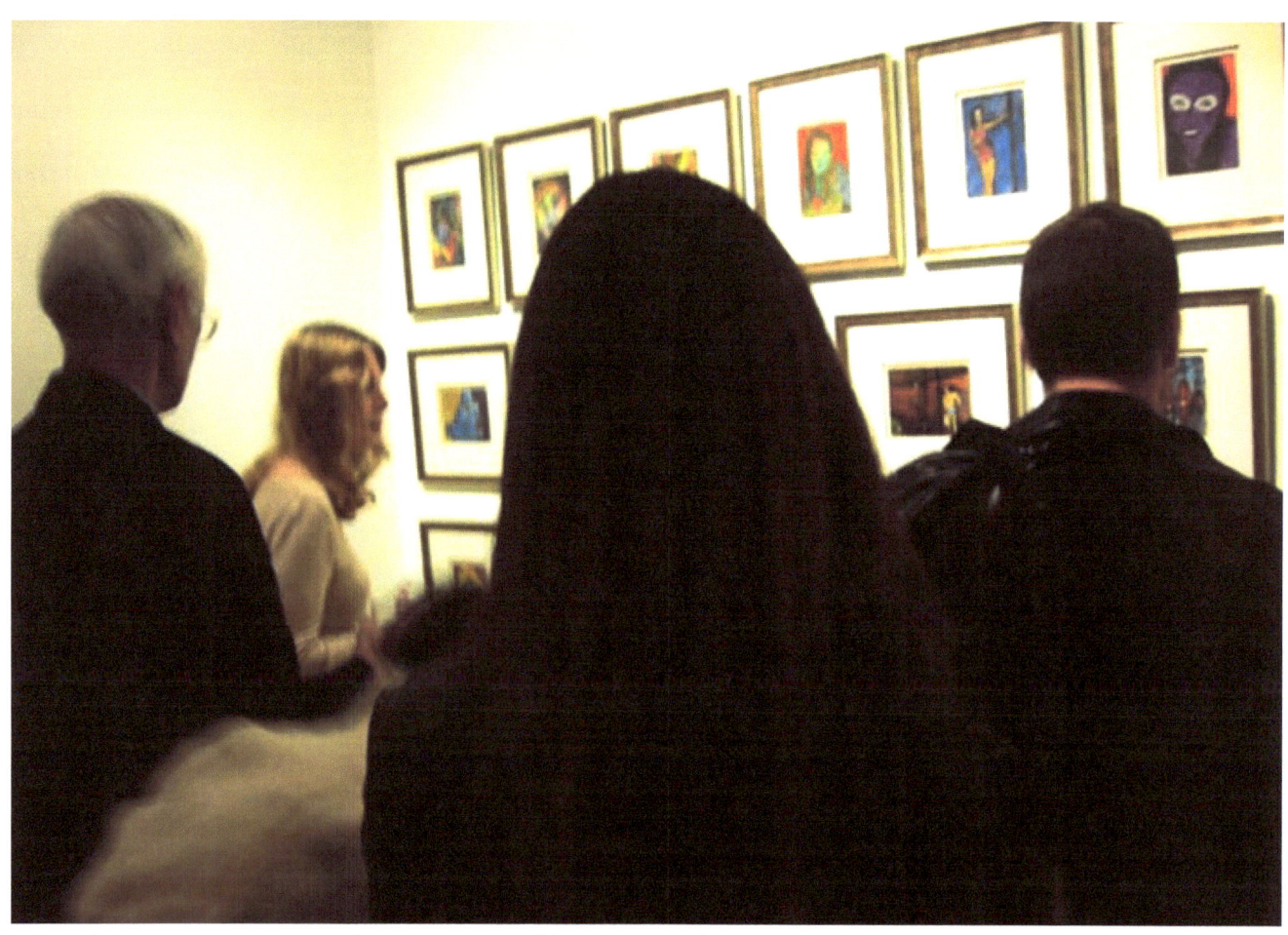

Before going to New York, I was worried how some of my paintings from the Bangkok Night might be perceived by some of New York's highly educated, politically active, very articulate professional women. However authentic my portrayal of the noir side of the Bangkok Night might be, would I be condemned for presenting such a nefarious (albeit colorful) world at all.

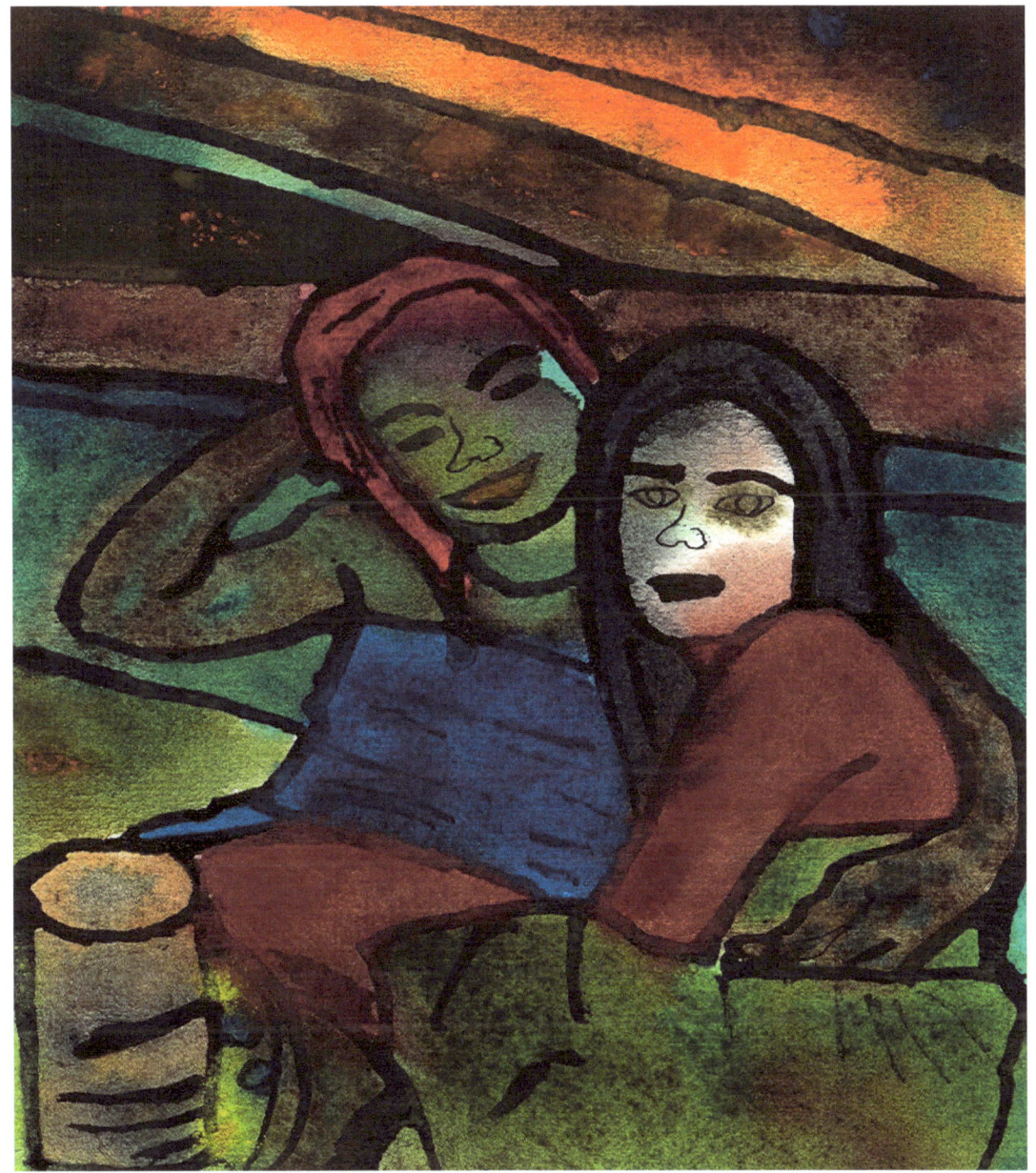

KTV Girls (water color on paper, 5x7 inch)

There must be more than ten thousand Karaoke Bars in Bangkok. The songs are stored on hard drives and delivered digitally. The whiskey and cola mixer comes on a stainless steel tray with a fresh bucket of ice. Tasty Thai snacks are cooked to order. Some KTV's are hi-end, others tucked in corrugated sheet metal sheds. There are usually some girls, to laugh, drink and sing with you or for you, smiling, flirting, mixing the drinks and ice. It's an instant party, so long as you have the cash to pay.

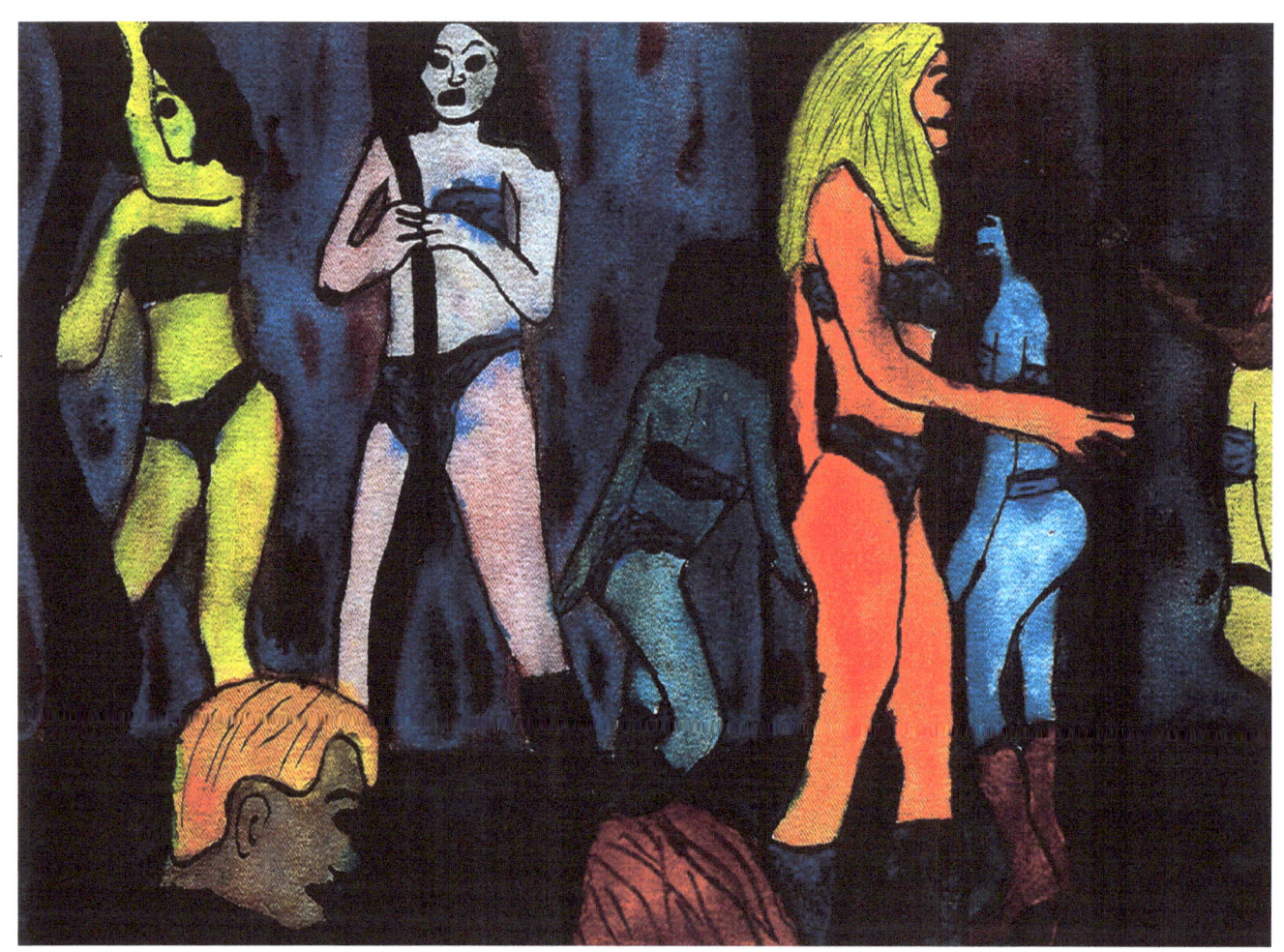

Rainbow Two Bar, (water color on paper, 7x5 inch)

Unlike most of Nana's bars, by ten o'clock, Rainbow One is full. The hundred or so girls are young and active, the guys old hands. They grab a beer, look around and find the girl they want. She comes over and orders a ladies drink. They check each other out. If everything's OK and both are willing, a few minutes later they're gone. By eleven, the bar's half empty.

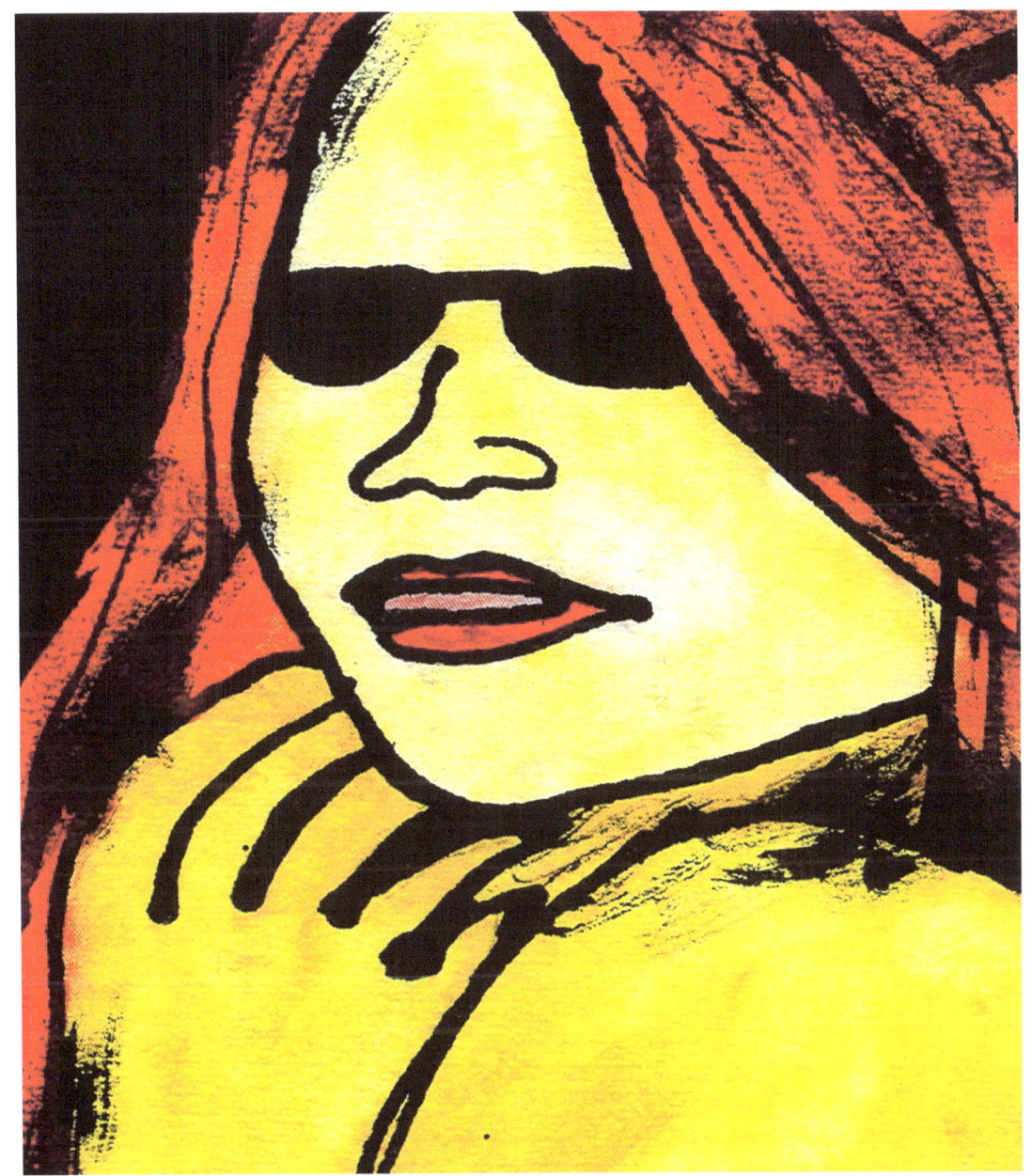

CM-2 Girl (water color on paper, 5x7 inch)

The girls at CM2 are a cut above, freelancers beholden to no one except themselves. Some are university students, others work at hotels, banks and department stores. The men they hunt are often high-income guys on business in Bangkok for a week. There's no upper limit. If they are stylish, clever and speak enough English, they can end up in London, Beverly Hills or Sydney, living in a big house and driving a Mercedes. Or they can end up no where, too old, with too much mileage, unloved, their dreams of a better life bitter and unfulfilled.

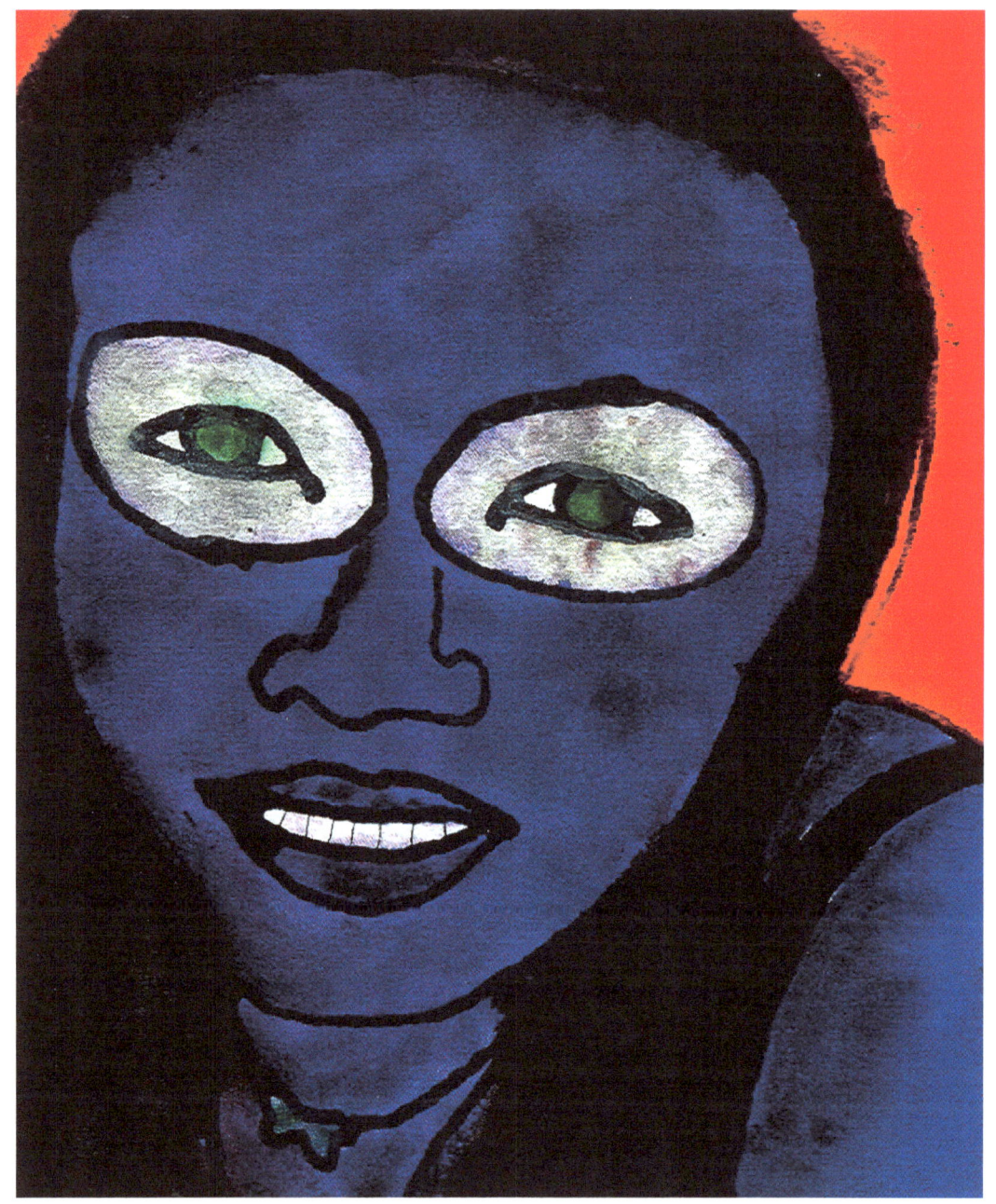

Butterfly Girl Q Bar (water color on paper, 5x7 inch)

Q Bar is ultra-chic. Club trance, guys dressed in Armani black, fashion model girls. Along with Living Room and Mystique, it's one of the top Bangkok clubs. But even in Q Bar, the boy-girl action is transactional and fast. No matter how wonderful the girls, how full of beauty, depth and soul, money determines the outcome, a pay as you go system with no obligations outside the time frame agreed.

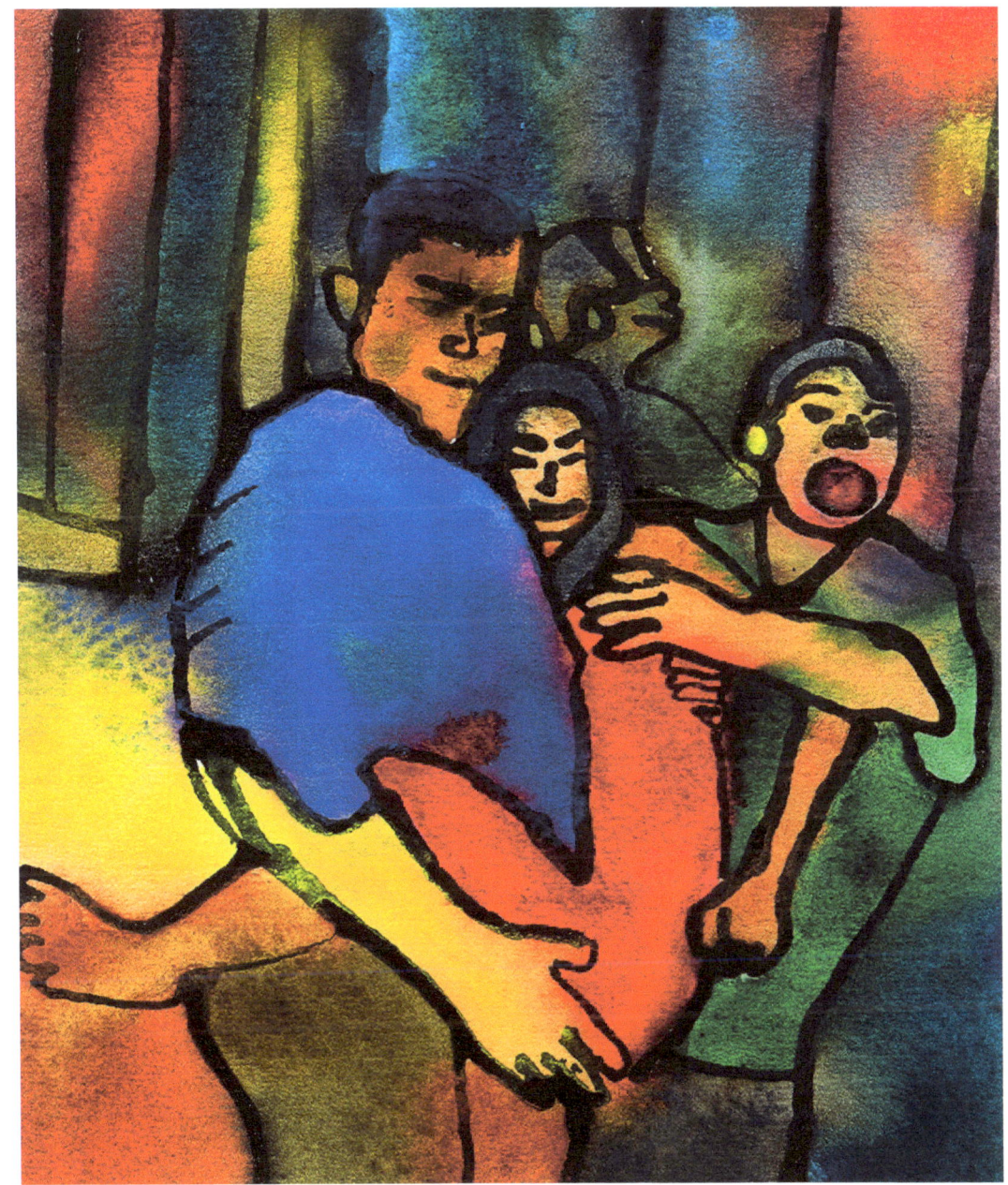

Midnite Bar Soi Cowboy (water color on paper, 5x7 inch)

One of the oldest bars on Soi Cowboy, Midnite's friendly and funky with a raunchy over-lay. The beers cost two dollars and the girls, mostly Lao from the part of Thailand called Isan, are easy-going, always looking for an excuse to be outrageous and have some fun. The guys, mostly Expats, some Japanese, think they're back in college, hanging out at a roadhouse bar for sex and rock 'n roll, the problems of their adult lives forgotten.

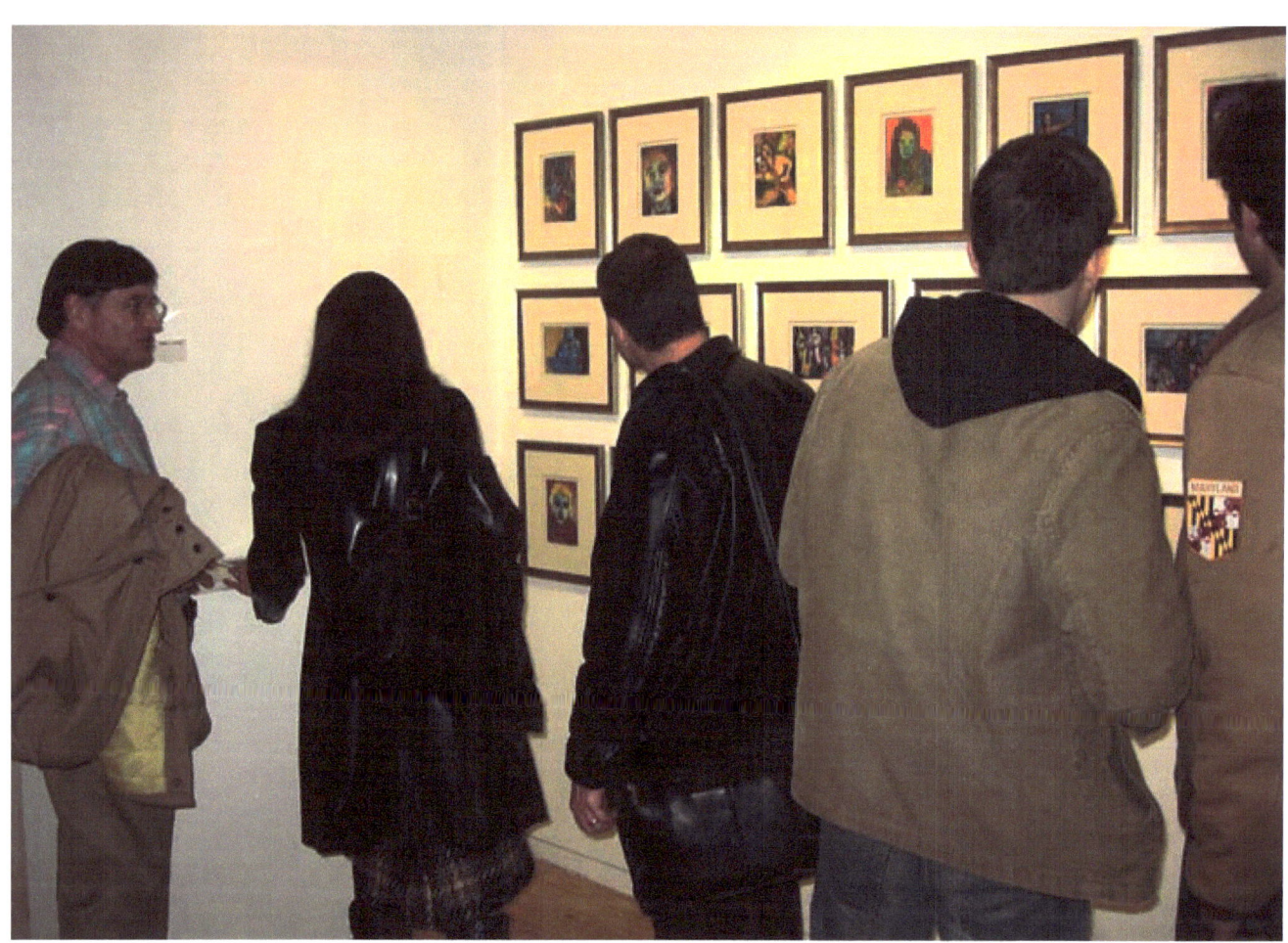

Altogther, the New York audience seemed to enjoy their glimpse into the Noir World of the Bangkok Night. Far away, different, strange, not really frightening considering the flight to get there is a long 24 hours. But will they ever feel comfortable putting the paintings in their living rooms? A few did...about ten of my Bangkok Night paintings reside in New York. But none in any of the museums yet!

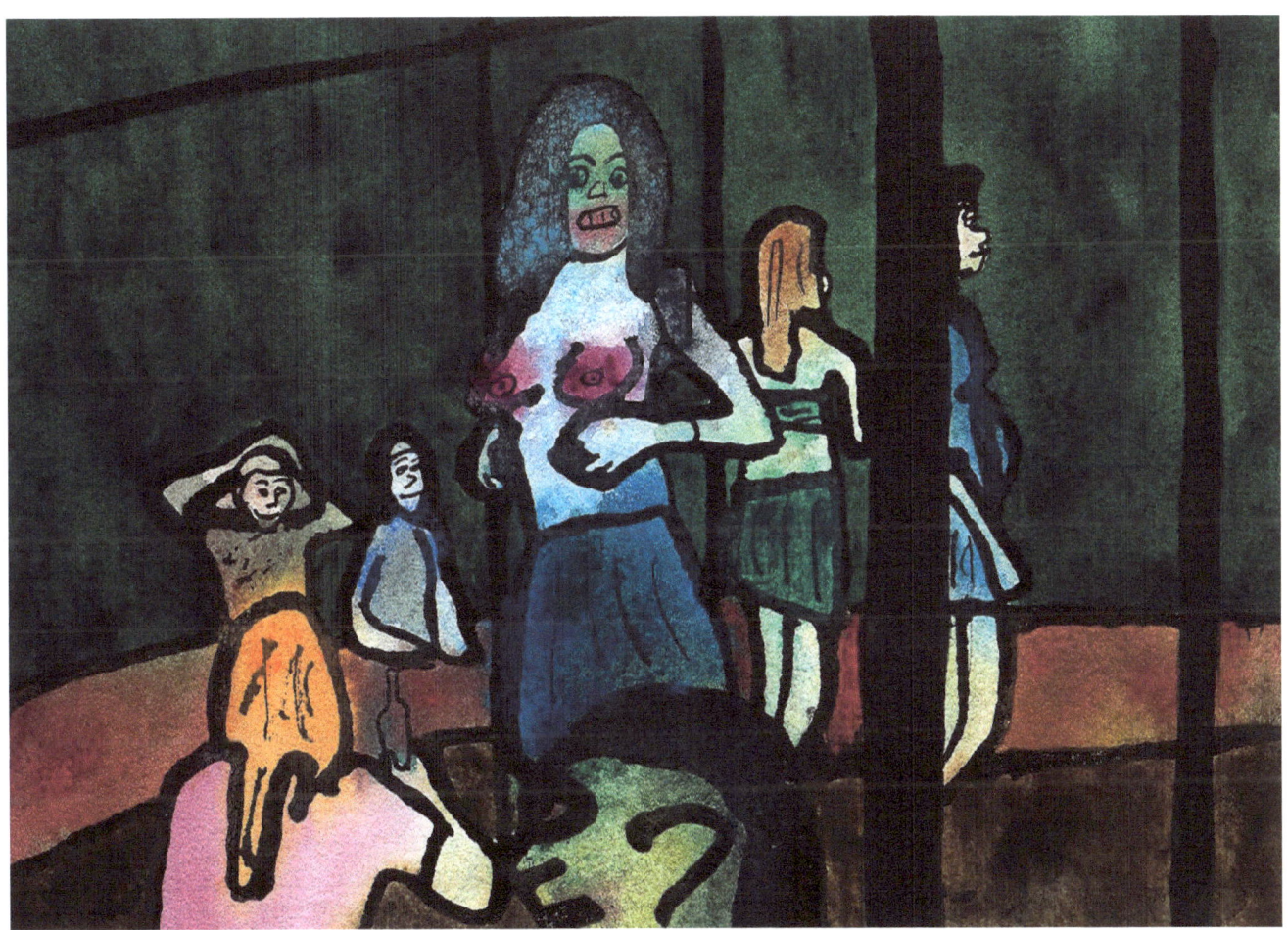

Quiet Night (water color on paper, 7x5 inch)

A quiet night in April, Bangkok's hottest month. Outside, even at midnight, it's a hundred degrees and a hundred percent humidity. Inside the bar, the A/C is on full blast, the beer cold and everybody's happy to go through the motions, thankful for the escape.

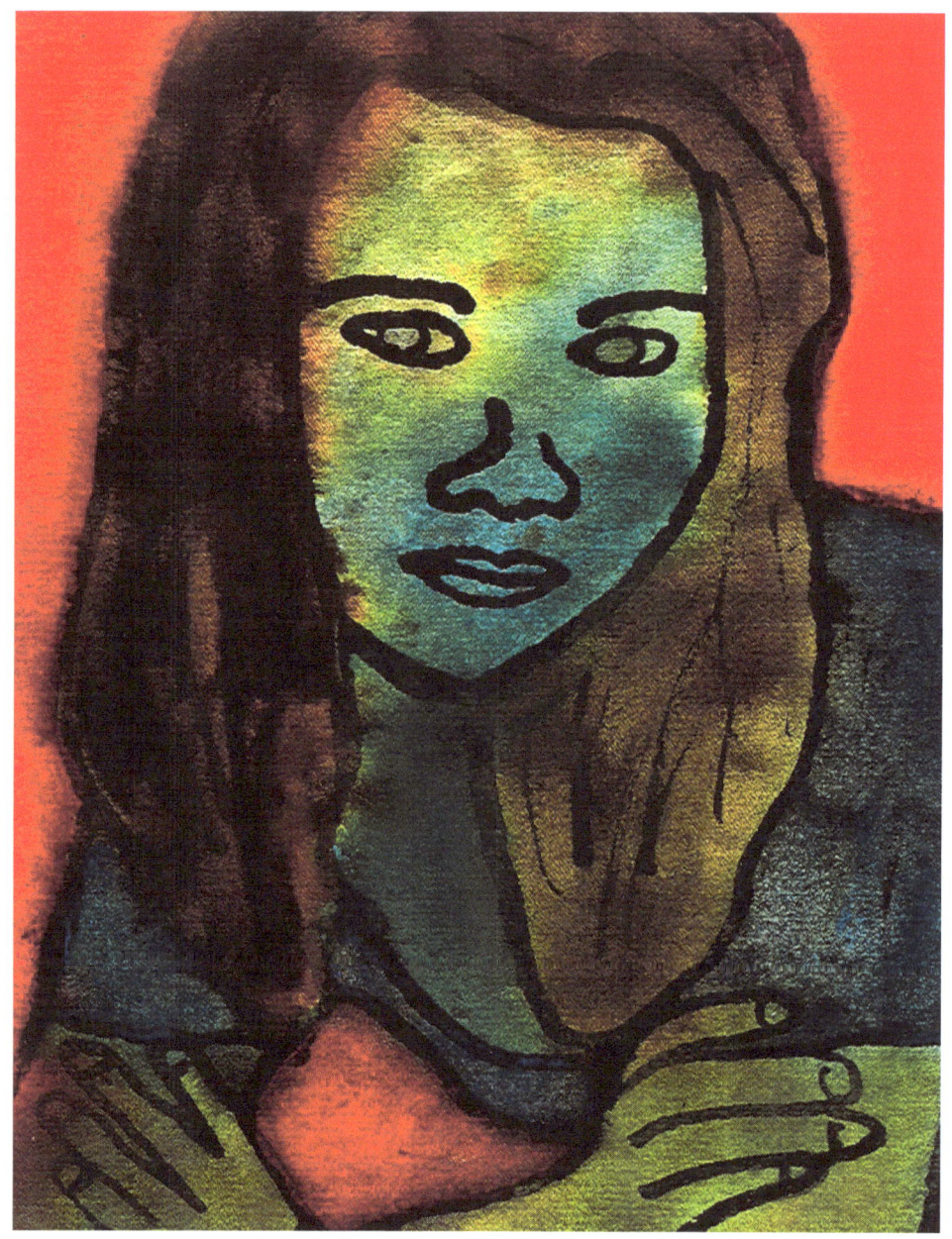

Kate (water color on paper, 5x7 inch)

Slender, stylish, often dressed in silk, her mini-mobile is always pressed to one ear, as her whispered Thai words flow across Bangkok's many-layered spectrum as she weaves her multiple webs. Her father, a Bangkok police captain, has a gun strapped to his ankle. When she was a teenage girl, he used to take her on nighttime tours of Chinatown to teach her the nature of Men. Before she reaches forty, she will be a dollar millionaire with an upscale Bangkok condo, a house in Sydney and a villa in Chiang Mai.

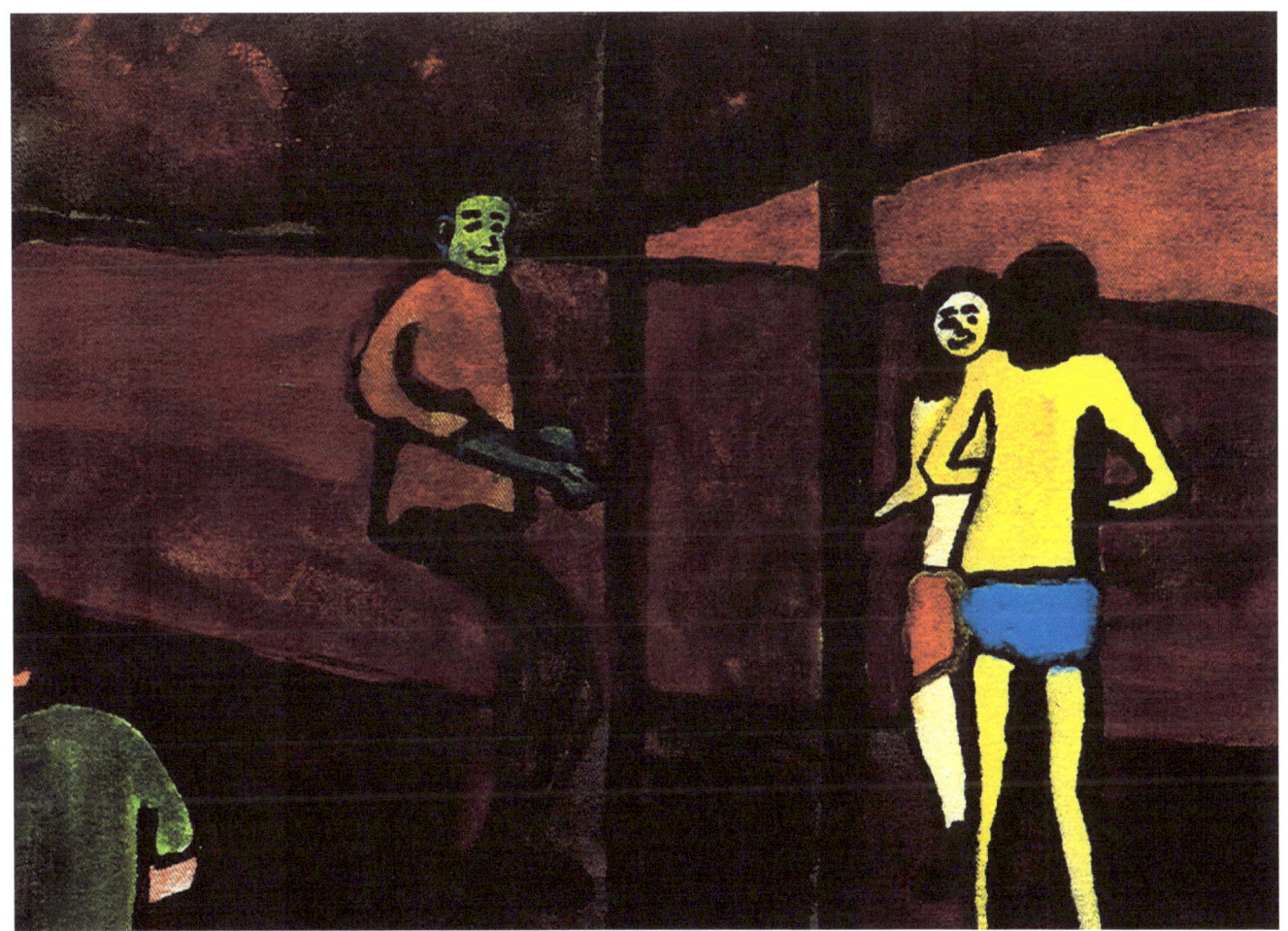

Closing Time Soi Cowboy (water color on paper, 7x5 inch)

The only customer's a friend, the last song is from the northeast part of Thailand called Isan. It's a tale of endless hard work on dirt-poor farms, the sons and daughters all lost to Bangkok to learn the ways of the City.

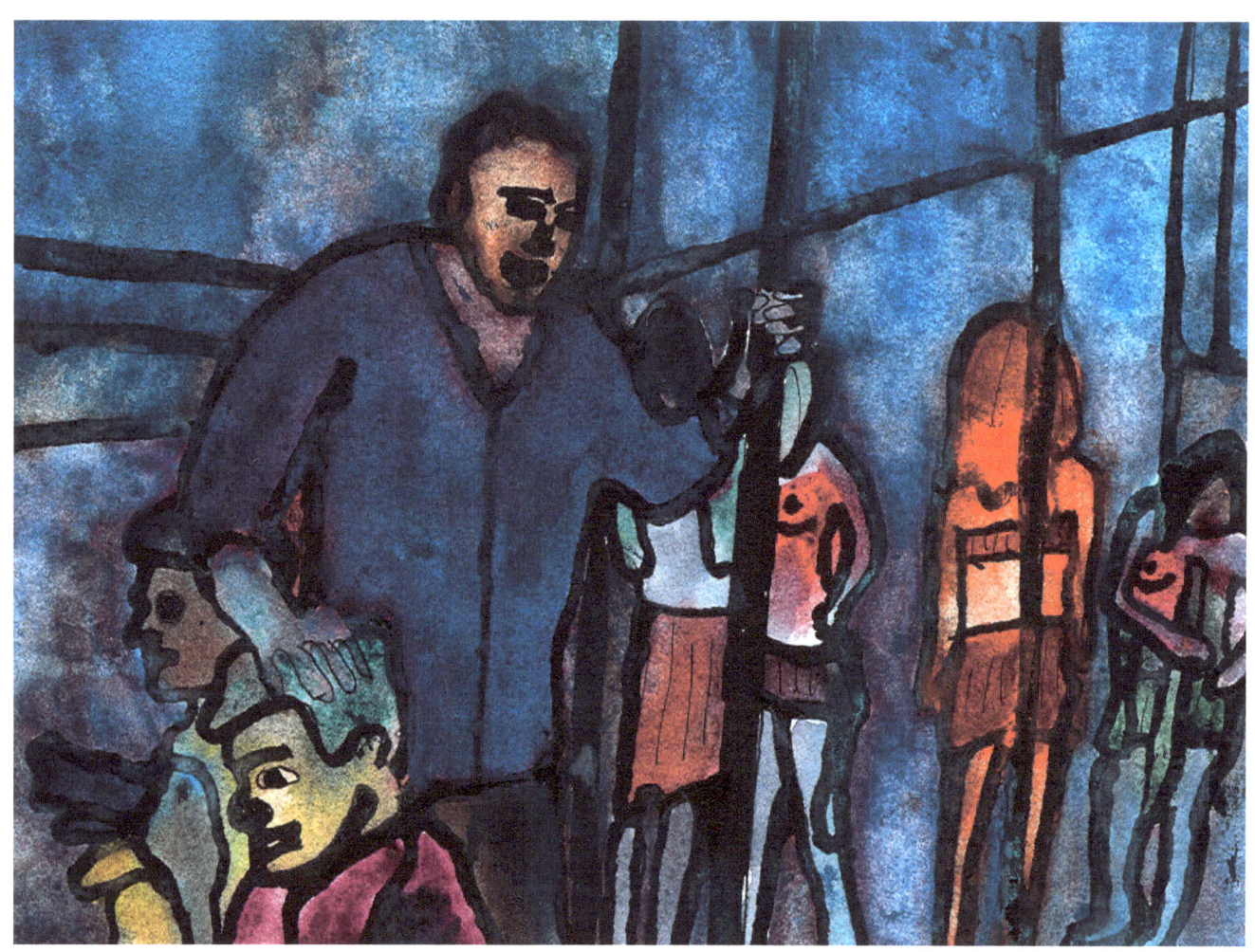

Closing Time Nana Plaza (water color on paper, 7x5inch)

The end of another night at Nana Plaza, the Expats all regulars and the leftover girls drifting through a haze of indifference.

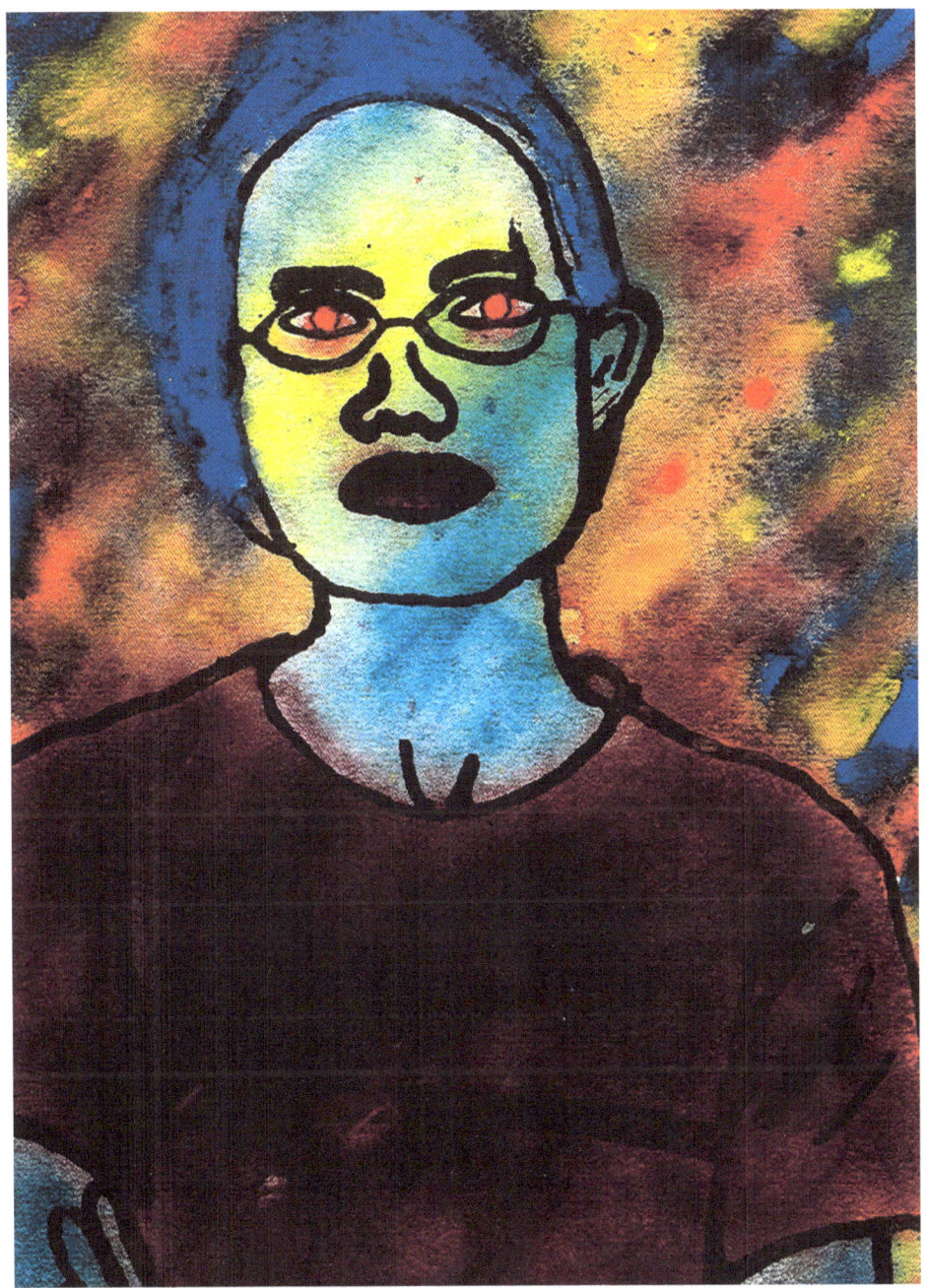

Om (water color on paper, 5x7 inch)

Once a month, she flies over to Hong Kong and works the disco in the Peninsula Hotel. She also works in Singapore. In between, she's at the CM2 Club at the Novotel Siam Square, a fire burning inside. In her next life, she wants to be a school teacher.

"The Bangkok Nights body of work expresses the raw power of humanity with both skill, concept and style of work. Influenced by German Expressionism, the paintings are the essence of pure emotion."
Angela Di Bello, Editor in Chief, ArtisSpectrum Magazine

"Chris Coles creates a noir world with surrealistic beings, splashed with bright colors, and drenched in atmosphere. He is one of the first artists to explore the scenes in Nana Plaza, Soi Cowboy, Patpong. His portraits look behind the mask of those in the scene. They are powerful and haunting images."
Christopher G. Moore, Author of the Calvino series of novels set in modern Bangkok

"Holy Frickin' WOW!!"
Tom Plate, Columnist, Singapore Times, South China Morning Post, Los Angeles Times

"Sexy and intriguing.............."
T.E.D. Klein, GQ Magazine Conde Nast

"Faites la tournée des lieux de vie nocturne - chic ou dirty, c'est selon - de Bangkok à travers la peinture expressionniste de Chris Coles, cet artiste amoureux de la Cité des Anges et grand explorateur du monde de la nuit. Du Bed Supperclub au Q-Bar, de Patpong à Soi Cowboy, du Mystique Club au Voodoo Bar, l'artiste vous emmènera, au gré de sa palette, dans l'univers enluminé, merveilleux et ensorcelant de Bangkok by night. Suivez le guide!"
Cyrsiam, Bangkok Romantic

"Chris Coles paints color drenched pop portraits rich in character. These mesmerizing works, simple line drawings bursting with deep color, appear at first glance digitally animated. They are a series of mixed media paintings inspired by Coles' keen observations of nightlife in Bangkok, Thailand. In an expressionist style of distorted line and clashing colors, the series follows in the footsteps of the German Expressionists painting nighttime Berlin in the early 1900's. 'The Bangkok Night is one of the greatest shows on earth,' Coles says. 'The clash of people and cultures, the raw and primitive display of humanity living on the edge.'"
Caroline Schwartz, Village Voice

Chris Coles Shows

Bergamot Station - Santas Monica 2005

Fritto Misto - Santa Monica 2006

Main Street Gallery - Santa Monica 2006

Agora Gallery - New York 2006

HHLT Gallery - Harpswell 2008

4th Street Gallery - Singapore 2009

Liam's Gallery - Pattaya 2009

Koi Gallery - Bangkok 2011

Bed Supperclub - Bangkok 2011

71 Prakanong - Bangkok 2011

FCCT - Bangkok 2012

Meta House Gallery - Phnom Penh 2013

Check Inn 99 - Bangkok 2015

Brainwake - Bangkok 2016

Check Inn 99 - Bangkok 2018

Meta House - Phnom Penh 2018

Hops Gallery - Phnom Penh 2018

Chris Coles Books

Navigating the Bangkok Noir

Bangkok Nights

Noir Nights in Phnom Penh

Bangkok Neon

Bangkok Noir in New York

One Night in Bangkok in Singapore

Kris Kolde in the Bangkok Night

Portraits from Bangkok

Patpong Portraits

Bangkok Noir in Pattaya

Colors of the Night

Night Visions

Paintings form the Phnom Penh Night

German Expressionism and the Bangkok Night

Flowers, One Butterfly and the Bangkok Night

Portraits from the Bangkok Night

Bangkok Noir at Check Inn 99

Pattaya Noir

www.ingramcontent.com/pod-product-compliance
Lightning Source LLC
Chambersburg PA
CBHW051824210526
45473CB00005B/1733